03 JUN 2009

944.04 REF

This book is to be returned on or before the date above.
It may be borrowed for a further period if not in demand.

ESSEX EDUC. COMM.
LIBRARY
No.
BILLERICAY SCHOOL
LIBRARIES

Heinemann

Heinemann Educational
Halley Court, Jordan Hill, Oxford OX2 8EJ
a division of Reed Educational and Professional
Publishing Ltd

OXFORD MADRID ATHENS FLORENCE PRAGUE
CHICAGO PORTSMOUTH NH (USA) MEXICO CITY
SAO PAULO SINGAPORE KUALA LUMPUR TOKYO
MELBOURNE AUCKLAND IBADAN NAIROBI
KAMPALA GABORONE JOHANNESBURG

© David Taylor 1997

The right of David Taylor to be identified as the author of this work has been asserted by him in accordance with the Copyright, Designs and Patent Act.

First published 1997
00 99 98 97
10 9 8 7 6 5 4 3 2 1

British Library Cataloguing in Publication data for this title is available from the British Library.

ISBN 0 435 31694 X

Designed by Ron Kamen, Green Door Design Ltd., Basingstoke. This edition produced by Celia Floyd.

Illustrated by Phill Burrows, Jeff Edwards, Jeremy Gowes, Tony Kenyon and Mark Peppé

Printed and bound in China

Front cover: 'Taking of the Tuileries, 10 August 1792.' Painted by Jean Duplessi-Bertaux (1747–1819); Chateau de Versailles.

Acknowledgements

The author and publisher would like to thank the following for permission to reproduce photographs:

Bibliothèque Nationale, Paris: 4.4B
Bildarchiv Preussischer Kulturbesitz, Berlin: 4.3B
Bowes Museum: 2.6D
Bridgeman Art Library: p.32, 1.1A, 1.3H, 1.3I
Bridgemen Art Library/Giraudon: cover
By courtesy of the Trustees of the British Museum: 2.5B, 2.7G, 3.1C, 3.7A, 4.1B, 4.4A, 4.4C
Bulloz: 2.4A, 2.8A
J. Allan Cash: 3.6C
Jean-Loup Charmet, Paris: 1.2C and p.35, 2.4B, 2.7F, 2.8D, 3.3C, 3.6A
C. M. Dixon: 3.4B
E. T. Archive: 2.2D, 2.6C, 2.7A, 3.2B
Garden Picture Library/Nigel Temple: 1.3J
Giraudon: 1.3A, 1.3C, 2.1A and p.34, 2.8B, 2.8C, 3.4F
Hubert Josse, Paris: 2.2A and p.35, 3.1A, 3.2C, 3.5A, 4.5B
S. and M. Matthews: 3.3B
Musée du Louvre/Christian Larrieu: 3.4A
Reunion: 2.7D, 3.5C

Every effort has been made to contact copyright holders of the material reproduced in this book. Any omissions will be rectified in subsequent printings if notice is given to the publisher.

Research help: Roger Butterworth

Details of written sources

In many sources the wording or sentence has been simplified to ensure that the source is accessible.

C. Barnett, *Bonaparte*, Allen and Unwin, 1978: 3.3A, 4.3D, 4.4D, 4.4E
Edmund Burke, *Reflections on the Revolution in France*, 1790, Penguin, 1982: 2.5A
R. Cobb and C. Jones (Eds.), *Voices of the French Revolution*, Salem House Publishers, 1988: 2.6A, 2.6B
L. Cowie, *Eighteenth Century Europe*, G. Bell, 1989: 1.3D
L. Cowie, *The French Revolution*, MacMillan, 1987: 1.3F, 1.3G
Michael Glover, *Napoleonic Wars*, Book Club Associates, 1979: 3.2E, 4.2B
Michael Glover, *Warfare in the Age of Bonaparte*, Book Club Associates, 1980: 3.2D
J. Hanoteau (H. Miles, Trans.), *Memoirs of General de Caulaincourt*, Duke of Vicenza, 1812-13, Cassell, 1935: 3.1B, 3.1E, 4.3A, 4.3C
J. C. Herold, *The Age of Napoleon*, Penguin, 1969: 3.2A, 3.5B, 3.6D, 3.6E, 4.1A
C. Hibbert, *Days of the French Revolution*, Penguin, 1989: 2.7B
R. M. Johnston (Ed.), *The Corsican, a Diary of Napoleon's Life in His Own Words*, Houghton Mifflin Co., 1910: 4.5A
C. A. Leeds, *European History, 1789-1914*, M and E Handbooks, 1989: 2.5C, 3.7B
Paul de Remusat (Ed.) (H. Miles, Trans.), *Memoirs of Madame de Remusat*, 1802-8, Sampson and Low, 1881: 3.1D
Emmanuel-Joseph Sieyes, *What is the Third Estate?*, 1789: 1.2
R. J. Unstead, *A History of the World*, A & C Black, 1983: 2.2B
B. Wright, *Revolution and Terror*, Longman, 1989: 2.2C

CONTENTS

PART ONE

1.1	Europe in 1780	4
1.2	The Three Estates	6
1.3	The Monarchy	8
1.4	The King in Debt and Danger	12

PART TWO   THE REVOLUTION

2.1	The Estates General	14
2.2	The Storming of the Bastille	16
2.3	1789 – The Year of Revolution	18
2.4	A New France	20
2.5	From Revolution to War	22
2.6	The Execution of the King	24
2.7	The Terror	26
2.8	Reaction	30
2.9	When was the Revolution?	32
2.10	Why was there a Revolution?	34

PART THREE   THE RISE OF NAPOLEON

3.1	Napoleon's Rise to Power	36
3.2	The Battle of Marengo	40
3.3	Invasion Britain	44
3.4	The New Caesar?	46
3.5	The Crowning of the New Caesar	48
3.6	The Great Reformer	50
3.7	Master of Europe	52

PART FOUR   THE FALL OF NAPOLEON

4.1	The Peninsular War	54
4.2	The Invasion of Russia	56
4.3	Retreat from Moscow	58
4.4	Defeat and Abdication	60
4.5	The Hundred Days	62
Index		64

1.1 Europe in 1780

Important countries

The most important countries in Europe in 1780 were **France**, **Prussia**, the **Habsburg Empire**, **Russia** and **Britain**.

Except for Britain, all of these countries were ruled by an **absolute monarch**.

What was an absolute monarch?

Ruled completely on their own

Did not believe in sharing power with a parliament

Absolute monarchs

Believed they had the power to do whatever they wanted

A portrait of Louis XVI in his coronation robes. Painted by a French artist.

Countries ruled by absolute monarchs

1 **France** In 1780 France was ruled by Louis XVI (1754–93). He ran the country on his own. There was no parliament. By 1789 he had become very unpopular with most of the French people. This was the year when the French Revolution started.

2 **Prussia** In 1780 Prussia (northern Germany) was ruled by **Frederick the Great** (1712–86). He, too, ran the country without a parliament. Frederick the Great fought many wars and made Prussia powerful.

Europe in 1780.

3 **The Habsburg Empire** Austria, Hungary and the Austrian Netherlands made up the Habsburg Empire (see map). In 1780 the Empire was ruled by **Joseph II** (1741–90). He also ruled without a parliament. Many people in the Empire did not like the way he ruled.

4 **Russia** This very big country was ruled by **Catherine the Great** (1729–96). She ruled without a parliament. The serfs (peasants) were treated badly. They rebelled in 1773. The rebellion was cruelly put down by the army.

A country not ruled by an absolute monarch – Britain

George III (1738–1820) was the British king in 1780. He was not an absolute monarch because he had to **share power with parliament**. Parliament made the laws. Britain was rich and powerful. It had a strong navy and a big **empire** in Africa and India. (When one country rules over other countries it has an empire.)

Questions

1 Look at the cartoon on page 4. Write down three things that an absolute monarch believed in.

2 a Which rulers in 1780 were absolute monarchs?
  b Which ruler in 1780 was **not** an absolute monarch? Explain why.

3 Look at **Source A**. How can you tell that Louis XVI thought himself to be very important?

1.2 The Three Estates

The French people were divided into three **estates** (groups).

First Estate	Made up of clergymen (bishops, abbots, priests)	130,000 in number
Second Estate	Made up of nobles (barons, dukes, counts)	400,000 in number
Third Estate	Made up of middle class (teachers, lawyers and merchants) and peasants	25,000,000 in number of which 20,000,000 were peasants

A SOURCE Nearly everybody is in the Third Estate. Yet all the well-paid government jobs are given to the bishops and nobles.

Written by a churchman in 1789 who thought that the Third Estate should be treated better by the king.

Unfair treatment!

The French people were treated very unfairly. For example, the members of the First Estate and Second Estate were given **special rights** by the king:

1 They did not have to pay much tax, although many bishops and nobles were very rich.
2 They were given jobs in the government by the king. So they had a say in the running of France.

The members of the Third Estate had **no rights** at all. They were forced to pay a lot of tax, but they had no say at all in the running of the country. This made the middle classes very angry.

But it was the 20 million peasants who suffered the most. They were very fed up with life.

B SOURCE The bishops spend huge sums of money on dogs, horses, furniture, servants, food and carriages. The priests are so poor they cannot afford to buy new clothes.

Written by a French priest of the time.

Taxes

The **taille** was a tax on wages or land. Only the Third Estate had to pay it!

In 1780 everyone needed salt to stop meat from going rotten. So the government put a tax on salt. It was called the **gabelle**.

People had to give one-tenth of their wages or crops to the church. This was called the **tithe**.

The hard life of a peasant

Did not own any land. Had to pay rent

Had to pay to use landlord's mill and oven

Had to pay a lot of tax to the government

Had to work for the landlord for nothing

A French cartoon drawn in 1789. The peasant is being crushed by a stone. 'Impots' were taxes and 'corvées' was forced labour.

Questions

1 Look at the chart on page 6. Who were members of
   a the First Estate
   b the Second Estate
   c the Third Estate?

2 Write down how many people were in each Estate.

3 Look at the cartoon. Write down two reasons why the peasants might have been unhappy.

4 Read **Unfair treatment**! Why were the middle classes angry?

C SOURCE

1.3 The Monarchy

Louis XIV and his family, painted in 1670. Louis is second from the left.

Three French Kings

Between 1643 and 1793 France was ruled by just three kings. All three were **absolute monarchs**. They made all the decisions. They did not believe in sharing power with a parliament.

King 1: Louis XIV (reigned 1643–1715)

Louis XIV was only four years old when he became the king. France was ruled for him by **Cardinal Mazarin**. He died in 1661 and Louis took charge of France.

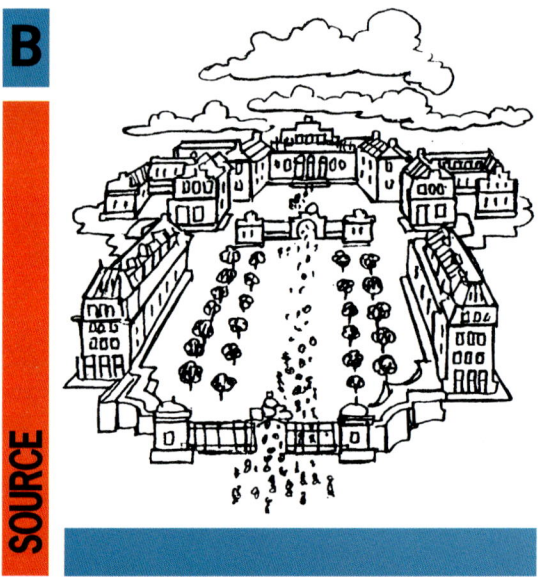

The Palace of Versailles built in 1661.

SOURCE C: Louis XIV's bedroom in the Palace of Versailles.

SOURCE D:

Louis XV's ministers tell him what to do.

His ministers do almost as they please.

Said by a French duke, 1747.

Most French people liked Louis XIV. He was clever and worked hard. His armies won many battles. Other countries were afraid of France at this time.

The Palace of Versailles

In 1661 Louis XIV ordered a huge palace to be built at Versailles, just outside Paris. Inside there were fine paintings, splendid decorations and beautiful furniture. It cost a vast amount of money to build.

Louis died in 1715. His wars and expensive living left France in **debt** (owing money).

King 2: Louis XV (reigned 1715–74)

Louis XV was five years old when he became the king. **Cardinal Fleury**, a clergyman, ran France until 1743.

Louis fought the Seven Years War (1756–63) against Britain. France lost and had a lot of its empire taken away. This made Louis unpopular.

Louis was also fond of spending money. France fell further into debt during his reign. The government was very short of money.

Questions

1. Read **Louis XIV**. Why did many French people like Louis XIV?

2. Read **The Palace of Versailles**. Why did Louis XIV leave France owing money?

3. Read **Louis XV** and **Source D**. Do you think Louis XV was a good king? Explain your answer.

King 3: Louis XVI (reigned 1774–93)

Louis XVI married **Marie Antoinette** in 1770. She was the daughter of Maria Theresa, the Empress of **Austria**.

The Petit Trianon

In 1774 Louis gave Marie Antoinette her own palace. It was called the **Petit Trianon**. She spent large amounts of money on it. In the grounds of the palace she built a garden with a lake, a theatre and a village.

Born to be a good king?

Louis was a large man with a big appetite. For breakfast he would eat four chops, a fat chicken, six poached eggs and a slice of ham. This was washed down with a bottle and a half of champagne!

Louis was kind to his family, but was also a ditherer. He found it hard to make decisions. He used to spend hours tinkering with his collection of clocks, rather than running the country.

E SOURCE

Louis XVI was not the right man to rule a country. He was shy and had no confidence. Others realized they could sway his decisions.

The view of a French nobleman.

F SOURCE

Louis XVI does have some common sense. He also has simple tastes and is honest.

This is his good side. He cannot make up his mind and is weak-willed. This is his bad side.

Written by a French monk in 1775.

G SOURCE

The French people were pleased at first when Louis gave the Trianon to the Queen.

They then became worried when they heard that she had built a garden costing £300,000.

The Queen has also bought many diamonds and she gambles at cards. She owes a lot of money.

Written by the Austrian ambassador at Versailles in 1776.

Questions

4 Read **Born to be a good king?** and **Sources E** and **F**. Make a large copy of the diagram and fill in the boxes.

Good Points — Louis XVI — Bad Points

5 Do you think Louis XVI was a strong king?

A painting of the Petit Trianon. You can see the gardens, lake and village built by Marie Antoinette.

The gardens at the Petit Trianon lit up at night.

One of the houses in the garden, still standing today.

Questions

6 Read **Source G** and look at **Sources H, I** and **J**.
  a What was the Petit Trianon?
  b How much money did Marie Antoinette spend on it?
  c What else did she spend money on?
  d French peasants had to give most of their wages in taxes. Why did they come to hate Marie Antoinette?

1.4 The King in Debt and Danger

Money problems!

By the mid–1780s Louis XVI had big money problems. Every year the government was spending more money than it had coming in (see diagram on page 13).

Why was Louis XVI in debt?

1 Costly wars

France had fought a lot of costly wars during the 18th century.

2 Heavy spending by the royal family

The French royal family had always been big spenders. The Palace of Versailles, for example, cost £30 million to build. Marie Antoinette spent large amounts on clothes, shoes and the Petit Trianon. She also had 500 ladies-in-waiting!

3 Not enough money was raised in taxes

The method of collecting taxes was both **unfair** and **inefficient**. The poor people who had the least money were taxed the heaviest. Those who could afford to pay lots of taxes – such as the nobles and bishops – paid hardly anything at all.

Things grew worse in the 1770s and 1780s when **bread prices were high** (see Source B). The poor had very little money left to pay their taxes.

Borrowing money makes the problem worse!

In the past, kings had always borrowed money to pay their way. This was a bad way of getting money because **interest** was charged on the loan (see Source A).

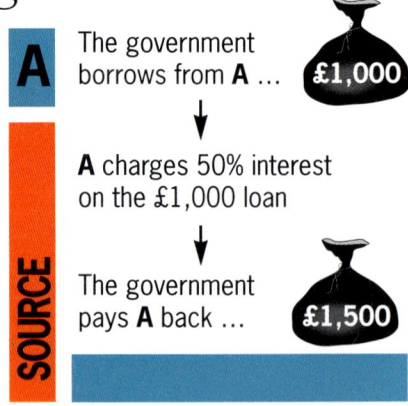

SOURCE A

The government borrows from **A** … £1,000

A charges 50% interest on the £1,000 loan

The government pays **A** back … £1,500

Interest on loans meant that more money was paid back than was borrowed in the first place.

The French Government had borrowed a huge amount of money. It could not afford to pay it back and run the country.

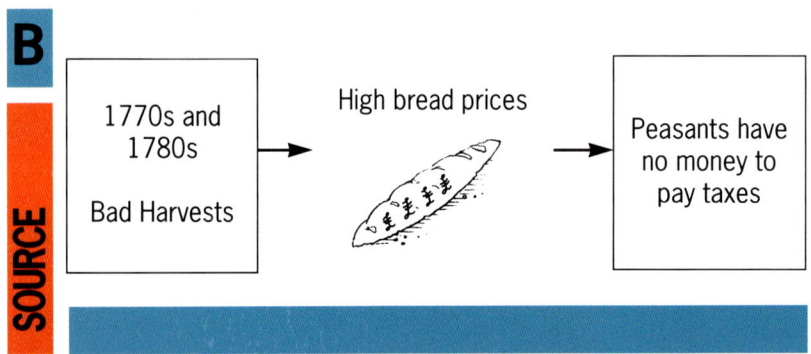

SOURCE B

1770s and 1780s Bad Harvests → High bread prices → Peasants have no money to pay taxes

High bread prices meant the peasants could not pay their taxes.

A dilemma

Louis knew that France would collapse if he did not pay off the money he owed. But borrowing more money to do this would only make things worse. What was to be done?

Government income and spending, 1786. (N.B. 1 French livre = £2)

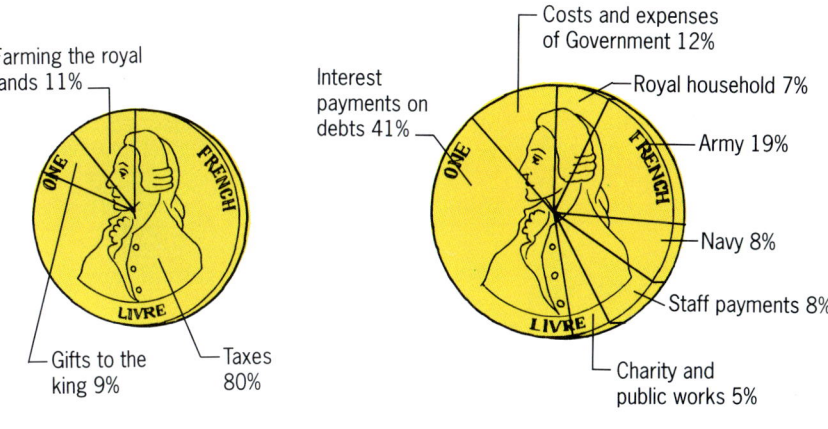

Income 472m livres (£944m)

- Farming the royal lands 11%
- Gifts to the king 9%
- Taxes 80%

Spending 633m livres (£1,266m)

- Interest payments on debts 41%
- Costs and expenses of Government 12%
- Royal household 7%
- Army 19%
- Navy 8%
- Staff payments 8%
- Charity and public works 5%

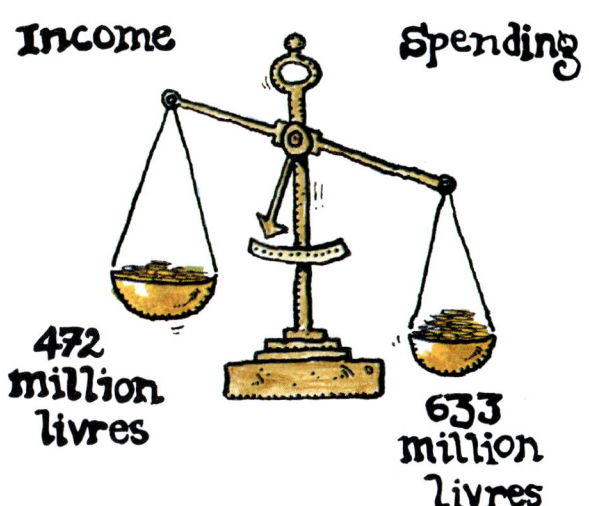

Income 472 million livres — Spending 633 million livres

Questions

1 Copy the cartoon below. Do the sum and fill in the sheet to say how much France had overspent in 1786.

2 a Read page 12. Copy and complete the chart below. Write one reason in each of the boxes.

Why Louis XVI was in debt
a
b
c

b Why was the method of taxing people a bad one?

3 Why was borrowing more money a bad idea?

2.1 The Estates General

Louis XVI tries to tax the rich

The best way to raise more money was to tax the rich (clergymen and nobles). They owned a lot of land. So Louis decided to put a **tax on land**.

Louis told to call the Estates General

The clergy and nobles did not want to be taxed. They told Louis he would have to call the **Estates General** to pass the new tax. The Estates General was a parliament made up of people from all three Estates. It had not met since 1614! Louis did not want it to meet. It might make trouble.

More problems – a food crisis

In July 1788 a huge hailstorm ruined all the cornfields. The harvest was poor. There was not much grain to make bread. Bread prices rocketed. By March 1789 a loaf of bread cost £1.50.

The poor could not afford such high prices. Thousands of peasants were starving. There were bread riots. Many peasants flocked to Paris in search of food.

The Estates General meets

Louis was a worried man. He was forced to call the Estates General. It met at Versailles on 5 May 1789. Louis hoped it would agree to the new land tax.

Calls for a constitution

Middle-class people in the Third Estate, such as lawyers and teachers, did not want to talk about taxes. Instead they asked for a say in the running of France. They said France should have a **constitution** (a list of rules for running the country). Louis did not like this idea. He was very angry.

Bread riots

Bad weather 1788

High bread prices

Violence and rioting by starving peasants broke out all over France.

A SOURCE

[Painting of the Third Estate making the Tennis Court Oath]

The Third Estate making the Tennis Court Oath. A painting by Jacques Louis David (see page 48).

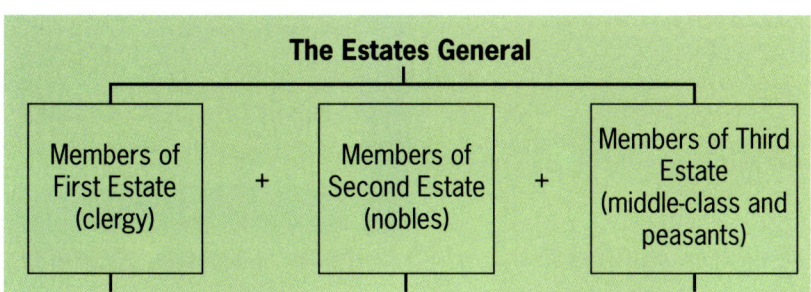

The Tennis Court Oath

Louis now tried to break up the Estates General. On 20 June 1789 the Third Estate went to a nearby tennis court and swore an oath. They said they would not go home until Louis agreed to a constitution.

The Third Estate also formed a new parliament called the **National Assembly**. On 27 June 1789 the clergy and nobles joined this Assembly.

Questions

Write out the passage below. Fill in the gaps.

The _____ and _____ would not agree to be taxed. Louis XVI was worried by the bread _____. He was forced to call a meeting of the _____ _____. It had not met since____. When it met the Third Estate said that France should have a _____ (list of rules). They swore the _____ _____ Oath. They said they would not go home until France had a _____.

2.2 The Storming of the Bastille

A The storming of the Bastille. This picture was painted soon after by a shopkeeper. He had taken part in the event.

Crowds gather in Paris

Thousands of working-class people gathered in Paris. They were angry.

Bread prices were still high. These people wanted to make their lives better.

Excitement mounts

Rumours started to go round that Louis XVI was going to get rid of the National Assembly. People did not want this.

Then Louis sacked a minister who was known to be on the side of the poor people. The crowd decided it was time for action!

B The fall of the Bastille was important. The Bastille stood for the power of the King over the poor.

Written by a historian in 1983.

C The fall of the Bastille meant the King was no longer in total control of France. It was the end of absolute monarchy.

Written by a historian in 1989.

D SOURCE

An engraving of 1789. It shows the storming of the Bastille.

The crowd marches on the Bastille

The Bastille was a big fortress in Paris. For years it had been used as a prison by the King. Anyone who complained about the king was locked up in the Bastille. The crowd was sure that it was full of prisoners.

On 14 July 1789 a crowd of 8,000 marched towards the hated Bastille. They wanted to destroy it. The King's soldiers did nothing to stop the crowd.

The Bastille falls

The crowd attacked the fortress. In the end the governor (head) of the Bastille handed over the keys. The crowd found just seven prisoners inside. They then cut off the governor's head.

A bad sign for Louis

The fall of the Bastille was a bad sign for Louis. For the first time the poor people of France had gone against the power of the king. In July and August peasants all over France attacked the rich and rioted. Louis was beginning to lose control of France.

Questions

1 Read **Excitement mounts**.
   a What was the rumour going around Paris?
   b What else did Louis XVI do to make the crowd angry?

2 Read **The crowd marches on the Bastille**.
   Why was the Bastille hated so much?

3 Read **A bad sign for Louis** and **Source C**.
   a Why was the fall of the Bastille a bad sign for the King?
   b What happened in July and August 1789?

2.3 1789 – The Year of Revolution

Louis loses control of Paris

Louis did think about using force to recapture the Bastille, but dropped the idea. He had now lost control of Paris.

The Great Fear

In July and August 1789 peasants in the countryside attacked the farms and houses of the nobles. The nobles were very scared. They called it the **'Great Fear'**.

New laws passed

The National Assembly did not like the violence. They passed laws which would help the peasants have a better life. They hoped this would stop the violence.

New laws passed by the National Assembly

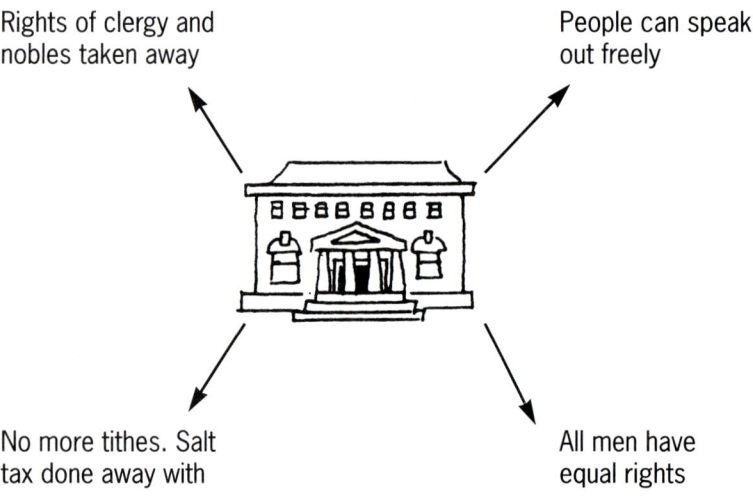

- Rights of clergy and nobles taken away
- People can speak out freely
- No more tithes. Salt tax done away with
- All men have equal rights

The march of the women

The violence did not stop. Louis would not agree to the new laws. Rumours started that the King was about to use soldiers to get rid of the National Assembly.

On 5 October an angry crowd of women marched to the Palace of Versailles. They told the King they could not afford the high price of bread. They brought the royal family back to Paris to live in the Tuileries Palace. The people could now keep an eye on the King.

Questions

1 **a** Make a large copy of this time-line.

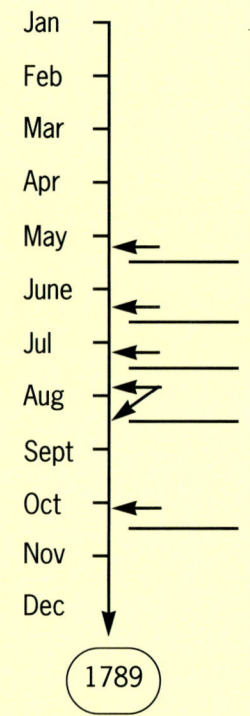

b Mark these events **in the right place** on your time-line (you will need to look back to Units 2.1 and 2.2):
- Fall of the Bastille
- March of the women to Versailles
- The Estates General meets
- The Great Fear
- The Tennis Court Oath

2.4 A New France

Changes in France

The National Assembly made many changes to the way France was run:

- The power of the king was reduced.
- The special rights of churchmen and nobles were taken away.
- Unpopular taxes, such as the salt tax (gabelle), were ended.

Not everyone liked these changes and soon there was more violence.

A new constitution

The National Assembly brought in a **constitution** – a set of rules for running France.
Louis XVI was told that he had to obey these rules. He now had to share power with the National Assembly. Louis did not like this because he was no longer in total charge of the country.

An inkwell showing a priest being crushed by the red cap of freedom. Red caps were worn by people who liked the Revolution. The idea for the red cap came from Ancient Rome. They had been worn by freed slaves.

SOURCE A

Changes made by the National Assembly 1789–91

- No one was allowed to be called a duke or baron anymore.

- Churchmen (such as bishops) now had to be **elected** (voted for). The king was not allowed to choose them anymore. They were under the control of the government.

- Land was taken away from the Church and became public property. Some of it was sold off to bankers, merchants and even peasants.

- Judges now had to be elected. They could no longer buy their jobs.

- New bank notes called **assignats** were brought in. They were used to pay off France's debts. However, this did not help the poor people.

Playing cards showing some of the changes in France. From 1790 there was:
- *freedom of the press (newspapers could print what they wanted)*
- *freedom of marriage*
- *equality of work*
- *equality of colour*
- *freedom of religion.*

Questions

1. Read **A new constitution**.
   a. What is a constitution?
   b. Why did Louis XVI not want a constitution?

2. Read **Changes made by the National Assembly 1789–91**.
   What changes were made to the Church?

3. Look at **Source A**.
   Why is the priest shown being crushed by a red cap?

2.5 From Revolution to War

The flight (escape) to Varennes – June 1791

Louis XVI did not want to share power with The National Assembly. So on 20 June 1791 Louis XVI and his family tried to escape from France. They could then get help from the Austrian Emperor (Marie Antoinette's brother). They reached the village of **Varennes** where they were stopped. They were taken back to Paris. People felt the King could no longer be trusted. They spat at the royal carriage.

Louis gets some help

The Austrian Emperor said he would help Louis win back the power he had lost. French **emigrés** (noblemen who had escaped from France) said they would form an army and invade France.

France declares war on Austria – April 1792

The National Assembly was worried. So in April 1792 it declared war on Austria. In July the Austrians invaded France. They beat the French army in two battles.

The September Massacres 1792

People began to panic. They thought Paris was about to be attacked. One working-class group which supported the Revolution was known as the *sans culottes* (meaning word for word *without knee breeches*). This was because they wore plain trousers, rather than breeches (which were worn by the nobles). They also wore red freedom caps.

The *sans culottes* murdered over 1,000 prisoners whom they thought were on the side of the Austrians. These killings were called the **September Massacres**. People in many other countries were disgusted. Cartoons like the one in Source B began to appear.

In November the French government passed the **Edict of Fraternity**. This said France would help people in other countries to have their own revolutions.

Ideas of the French Revolutionaries

1 **Liberty** [all people were born free]

2 **Equality** [all people were born equal]

3 **Fraternity** [brotherhood and friendship between people]

A SOURCE

Would our monarchy be done away with? Would bishops be got rid of?

Would titles such as 'duke' be ended? Would law and order break down?

Edmund Burke, an Englishman, writing in 1790. Burke was worried about what might happen if Britain had a Revolution.

B SOURCE

Un petit Souper, a la Parisienne; — or — A Family of Sans Culotts refreshing, after the fatigues of the day.

A cartoon by James Gilray, 1792. Gilray was English. He drew this just after the September Massacres.

C SOURCE

[In 1792] there was a food shortage in France. Many people were out of work. Law and order broke down.

C. A. Leeds, a historian, 1989.

Questions

1 Read **The flight to Varennes**.
   a Why did Louis XVI try to escape from France?
   b Describe what happened.

2 Read **Louis gets some help**.
   a Who was willing to help Louis?
   b Why would they want to help Louis?

3 Read **The September Massacres**.
   a Who were the *sans culottes*?
   b Why did they kill over 1,000 prisoners?

4 Look at **Source B**.
   a What did Gilray want people to think about the *sans culottes*?
   b Why do you think he wanted them to think this?

5 Read **Source A**. Why would an Englishman be worried about what was happening in France?

THE FRENCH REVOLUTION 23

2.6 The Execution of the King

Events leading to the King's execution

1. Louis XVI disliked having to share power with a parliament.

2. On 20 June 1791 he tried to escape from France (see page 22). He was brought back to Paris.

3. In April 1792 the Austrians invaded France. Many people thought Louis wanted this to happen. They said he was a traitor. On 10 August an angry crowd attacked the Tuileries Palace.

4. Louis was put in prison. On 21 September 1792 a new parliament (**The National Convention**) made France into a republic (a country without a King).

5. Louis was put on trial and found guilty of plotting against France. He was sentenced to death.

6. Louis was executed in Paris on 21 January 1793.

A SOURCE

His blood flows. Many people dip a fingertip in the blood. One even tastes it. One of the executioners sells bundles of his hair. People buy the ribbon that tied it.

Everyone goes around, arm in arm, laughing and talking as if they are at a festival.

Cakes are sold around the body. The body was put in a wicker basket, just like a common criminal.

A description of Louis XVI's execution by a person who wanted France to be a republic. This person saw the execution.

B SOURCE

Right to the end Louis XVI was full of courage. In a strong voice he said:

'I forgive my enemies. I trust my death will be for the happiness of the people. But I fear France may suffer from the Lord's anger.'

The King took off his coat. He walked on to the scaffold with a firm, brisk step.

After his death his body was thrown into a pit, fifteen feet deep. There it was burned.

Nothing now remains of this unhappy king. Only the memory that he was a good, but unlucky, man.

Written by a supporter of the King, 23 January 1793.

C

Engraving of the execution of Louis XVI. It is not known who painted it or when it was painted.

D

A plate showing the execution of Louis XVI. It was made soon after the execution.

Questions

1 Read **Events leading to the King's execution**.
   a When was Louis executed?
   b Why was he executed?
   c What is a republic?

2 Source A makes it sound as if people were happy to see Louis XVI die. Source B does not mention this. It says Louis was brave and unlucky.
   Why do you think these two sources say different things?

2.7 The Terror

More countries declare war on France

The execution of Louis XVI horrified people in other countries. Austria, Prussia, Spain, Sardinia, Holland and Britain all joined together to fight France. They were too powerful for France and beat the French armies.

The Reign of Terror

Between 1793 and 1794 many people who were thought to be against the Revolution were executed. This time was known as the **Reign of Terror**.

Causes of the Reign of Terror

The National Convention (government) was worried, so it started the Reign of Terror.

1. They thought that **royalists** (supporters of the King) were passing information to the enemy.
   This was why the French armies were beaten.
2. Royalists in western France rebelled against the government. Many people were killed.
3. Bread prices were very high. People began to steal bread from shops. Law and order was breaking down again.

A SOURCE

A painting of a courtroom, 1794.

B Examples of 'crimes' for which people were executed during the Reign of Terror.

- Jean Julien, a wagoner, was given twelve years hard labour. He called out 'long live the King'. He was brought back and sentenced to death.

- Henriette Marbouef was found guilty of keeping food for the Austrians and Prussians. She was executed.

- Marie Plaisant was found guilty of saying she was not bothered about France. She was executed.

SOURCE

From the Execution Record, 1793.

The threat to the revolutionary government in 1793.

The Committee of Public Safety

This Committee was set up in April 1793. It was made up of a group called the **Jacobins**, whose leader was **Maximillian Robespierre**. They wanted to get rid of anyone who was thought to be against the Revolution. Source B shows how the courts could find many reasons to put people to death.

Questions

1 Read page 26.
  a What was the Reign of Terror?
  b Why was it started?

Executions galore!

The Committee of Public Safety said that the Terror was needed to rid France of royalists. About 3,000 executions took place in Paris and 14,000 in the rest of France.

- In **Paris** thousands of people watched the executions. The **guillotine** was used to behead people. Women did their knitting as they sat watching. Marie Antoinette was guillotined in October 1793.
- In Nantes 2,000 people were drowned in the river Loire. Birds flocked to eat the rotting flesh.
- In Lyons an official said the guillotine was too slow. So he had 300 people shot by cannon fire. (See the map on page 27.)
- One of the revolutionary leaders said that they had to punish not just traitors, but also the people who did not care one way or the other (see source B on page 26).

A change in mood

People's mood soon changed. They became frightened. There were so many executions people started to worry that they would be the next to go.

People turned on Robespierre. He was blamed for all the killings. On 27 July 1794 Robespierre was arrested in the town hall in Paris.

The dreaded guillotine.

A sketch of Marie Antoinette on the way to the guillotine, 16 October 1793.

The Terror is ended

On 28 July 1794 Robespierre was executed by the guillotine. After this prisoners were freed. The Terror was at an end.

SOURCE E

People were taken to the guillotine in tumbrils (carts).

SOURCE G

A British cartoon of 1793, showing the Reign of Terror.

SOURCE F

Robespierre is shot in the jaw during the struggle to arrest him.

Questions

3 Read **Executions galore!** Copy the chart below and fill in the spaces.

The Reign of Terror	
Place	Number executed
Paris	
Rest of France	

4 Read **A change in mood**. Why did people become worried about the Terror?

5 Read **The Terror is ended**. What happened to Robespierre?

2.8 Reaction

Paris becomes more peaceful

When the Reign of Terror ended in July 1794 things became quieter. People started to enjoy life again.

In Paris the restaurants and cafés re-opened. Those who could afford it could eat out.

The poor had to eat the left-overs which were thrown out from the kitchens. Some of the 'new' poor were noblemen who had survived the Revolution but had lost everything.

Gambling and dancing

Gambling clubs and the theatre became popular again. There was also a new craze for dancing.

Changes in Fashions

During the Revolution people had worn simple clothes. The *sans culottes*, for example, wanted to show that they believed in equality (see Source A). People also stopped putting powder in their hair.

Now some people started to dress in outrageous clothes. Young men, called ***incroyables***, led the way (see Source D). Their hair was short at the front and long at the back. The *incroyables* could be seen walking in the gardens of the Tuileries.

The main change in fashion was that people now liked to copy the styles of the ancient Greeks and Romans. The red cap of liberty (freedom) became very popular in France. Red caps had first been worn by freed Roman slaves. If people wore a red cap in the 1790s it showed that they supported the Revolution.

The sans culottes. 'Sans culottes' means 'without knee breeches'.

SOURCE A

The *sans culottes* showed their support for the Revolution by rejecting the knee breeches and silk stockings of the nobles. Instead they wore plain trousers, short jackets, a scarf around the neck and a liberty cap. The women dressed with similar simplicity.

B *An example of women's fashion before the Revolution.*

C *Women's fashions after the Revolution copied the styles of ancient Greeks.*

D *An incroyable in 1795. They wore outrageous clothes.*

Questions

1. Read **Paris becomes more peaceful** and **Gambling and dancing**.
   How did people celebrate the end of the Terror?

2. Read **Fashions**.
   Why did the *sans culottes* wear plain trousers and red caps?

2.9 When was the Revolution?

Chain of Events

Assembly of Notables:
spring 1787

Floods, poor harvest, riots:
autumn–winter 1788–89

Meeting of Estates:
May 1789

Tennis Court Oath:
June 1789

Storming of the Bastille:
July 1789

Peasant uprisings:
July–August 1789

End of nobles' rights:
August 1789

March to Versailles:
October 1789

End of nobles' titles:
1790

Royal family escapes.
Captured at Varennes:
June 1791

War with Austria:
April 1792

Crowd attack King at Tuileries:
August 1792

September Massacres:
September 1792

Edict of Fraternity:
November 1792

King on trial:
December 1792

Execution of King:
January 1793

Jacobins seize power:
April 1793

What is a Revolution?

A 'revolution' is when the way of running a country is changed. The change happens quickly and often there is violence.

The French Revolution changed the way France was run. This change happened very quickly.

Monarchy to republic – how the Revolution changed France

1. France was run by a king without a parliament.

    this changed...

2. The King was made to share power with a parliament.

    this changed...

3. The King was put in prison. France became a **republic**. There was a parliament but no king. The King was executed in 1793.

When did the French Revolution begin?

Which event started the French Revolution?
It is hard to pick on any one event alone and say it was the start of the Revolution.

As a result, historians have different opinions about this. Some of these opinions are shown in Sources A, B and C.

The view of historian 1.

The view of historian 2.

The view of historian 3.

Questions

1. Using the **Chain of Events** say whether things grew better or worse for Louis XVI between 1789 and 1793.

2. Look at **Sources A, B** and **C**.
    a. Make a large copy of the chart opposite.
    b. Fill in the opinion of each historian about when the Revolution started.
    c. Which event do **you** think started the Revolution?

Person	Event which started the Revolution
Historian 1	
Historian 2	
Historian 3	

2.10 Why was there a Revolution?

Historians are very interested in **why** something happens. They look for reasons – these are called **causes**.

Causes are what help to make something happen.

In this unit five different causes of the French Revolution are shown in the pictures. (Note: these are not the only causes of the Revolution.)

Some causes happened during 1789. These are called **short-term** causes because they happened **just before** the event.

Other causes had been **going on for many years** before the event. These are called **long-term** causes.

Some causes are more important than others. Historians do not always agree which causes are the most important.

The kings of France lived a very rich lifestyle.

The Third Estate swore the Tennis Court Oath on 20 June 1789. They wanted a say in the running of France.

Questions

1 Look at the causes of the French Revolution shown on these pages.

2 Decide which are short-term and which are long-term causes.

3 Make a large copy of the diagram. Write the causes into the right boxes.

Long-term cause	1
Long-term cause	2
Long-term cause	3
Short-term cause	4
Short-term cause	5

↓

The French Revolution

Causes of the French Revolution

The poor people also wanted change. They stormed the Bastille on 14 July 1789.

The bishops and nobles lived well, but life had always been hard for the peasants.

The King had been in debt for many years.

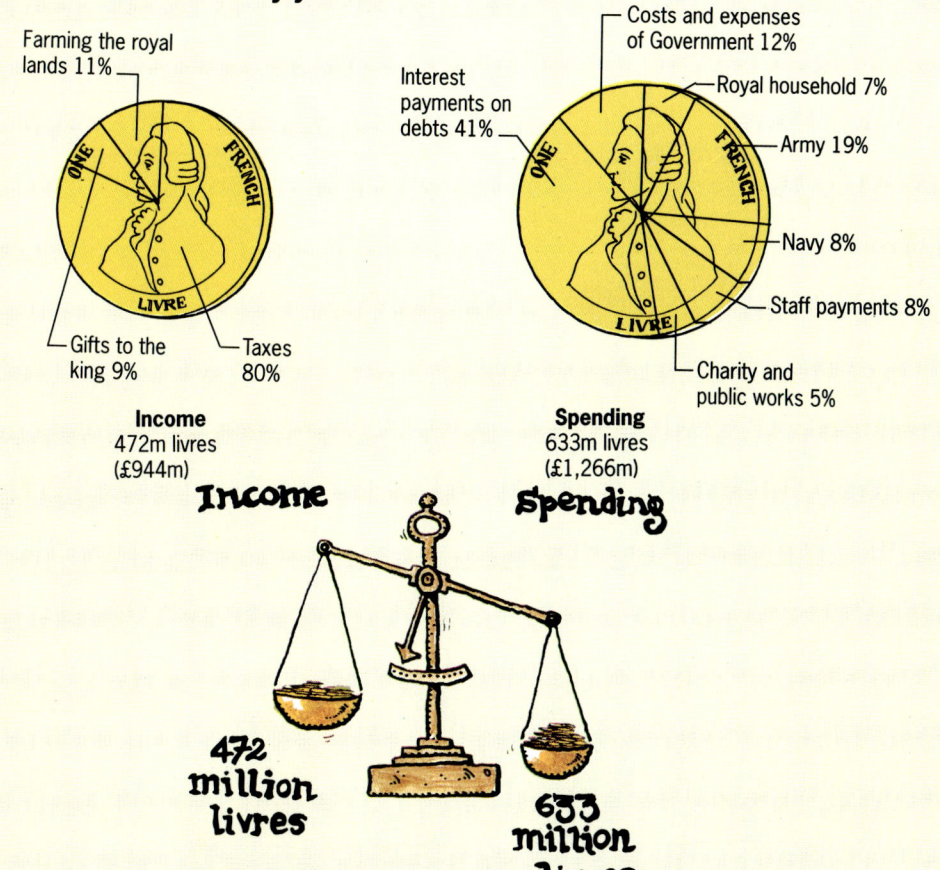

Farming the royal lands 11%
Gifts to the king 9%
Taxes 80%

Income
472m livres
(£944m)

Interest payments on debts 41%
Costs and expenses of Government 12%
Royal household 7%
Army 19%
Navy 8%
Staff payments 8%
Charity and public works 5%

Spending
633m livres
(£1,266m)

Income — 472 million livres
Spending — 633 million livres

3.1 Napoleon's Rise to Power

Napoleon's early life

Napoleon Bonaparte was born in Corsica in 1769. His father was a lawyer.

At school Napoleon was good at science and mathematics.

In 1784 he went to a military school. In 1785 he joined the French army.

The siege of Toulon

Toulon is a port in the south of France. In 1793 Toulon was captured by the British. Napoleon was in charge of some French army gunners. He forced the British out of Toulon.

The revolutionary Government (now known as the **Directory**) was very pleased with Napoleon. It was not long before he was made a Major General.

> ### The Directory
> In July 1794 after the death of Robespierre a new group took over the government of France. This group was called the **Directory**.

The Battle of the Pyramids, painted by a French artist in 1810 (see next page.)

SOURCE A

More success for Napoleon

In 1796 France was fighting the Austrians in Italy. Napoleon won a number of battles for the French. He returned to Paris a hero.

The Egyptian campaign

Britain was still at war with France. Britain had conquered land in India. Napoleon said if the French captured Egypt, they would be able to stop Britain trading with India.

The Battle of the Pyramids

In 1798 Napoleon's army set sail for Egypt. Napoleon beat the Egyptians in a hard fought battle known as the **Battle of the Pyramids**.

People in France thought Napoleon was very brave. Paintings such as Source A, showing him as a hero, were very popular.

The British hit back

The British sent a fleet of ships to Egypt. It was commanded by **Lord Nelson**. The British navy beat the French navy in the **Battle of Aboukir Bay**.

The French soldiers then fell ill with the plague. Things were not looking so good for Napoleon now.

The Egyptian campaign and other battles of Napoleon's career.

Napoleon returns to France

Napoleon heard that the Directory (see page 36) had become unpopular in France. In October 1796 he secretly left his army and went back to Paris.

He thought he could win power for himself. He was asked to join a plot to overthrow the Directory.

> **SOURCE B**
>
> Napoleon would pay any price for success.
>
> Napoleon once said: 'I would kiss anyone's foot, if I needed them.'

Said by one of Napoleon's closest friends.

Napoleon seizes power

Napoleon was able to take power because:

- There was a shortage of food in France. People blamed the Directory.

- Prices were very high and people were poor. They blamed the Directory.

- People wanted a strong leader to bring peace. They were tired of war.

- The people looked up to Napoleon as a hero.

SOURCE C

The Corsican Crocodile dissolving the Council of Frogs!!!

A British cartoon showing Napoleon seizing power.

38 THE FRENCH REVOLUTION

The Directory is overthrown

On 9 November 1799 Napoleon and his soldiers went to the building where the Directory was meeting.

They frightened the members of the Directory. They fled for their lives.

A new government for France

Three **consuls** (officials) were now put in charge of France. They had the power to make laws. One of the consuls was Napoleon. He was soon telling the other two consuls what to do!

SOURCE D

Napoleon talked to his soldiers about their wounds and the battles they had fought in. He knew the names of his soldiers and gave them a cheering word.

He spoke to his men in a friendly voice. The soldiers liked this and would follow him anywhere.

Written by a friend of Josephine, Napoleon's first wife.

SOURCE E

I was very careful. I took advice from everyone. When I became a consul everyone was curious to see me. Everyone in France was pleased.

Napoleon talking about the overthrow of the Directory.

Questions

1 Draw a time-line using the events below:

   1793 Siege of Toulon
   1798 [July] Battle of the Pyramids
   1798 [August] Battle of Aboukir Bay
   1799 Napoleon overthrows the Directory

2 Underline the events which were a **success** for Napoleon.

3 Read the box called **Napoleon seizes power**. Why was Napoleon able to overthrow the Directory?

3.2 The Battle of Marengo

Austria and France

Ever since 1792 France had been at war with Austria. Louis XVI's wife, Marie Antoinette, had been Austrian. Many people in Austria were sorry about what had happened to the French royal family and the nobles. The Austrians did not like Napoleon. They saw him as a threat to their country.

Napoleon aims to beat Austria

Napoleon thought it would make him even more popular with the French if he beat the Austrians.
In 1800 Napoleon decided to attack the Austrian army in Italy. The French army crossed the Alps through the Great St Bernard Pass.

The Marengo campaign.

SOURCE A

It took the French army five days to travel through the Great St Bernard Pass.

It was a hard journey for the 40,000 men. They had to carry all their baggage and make sure the guns got through.

The journey was organized by General Berthier.
The soldiers and the mules also deserved a lot of praise.

Napoleon rode on a mule.

Written by a historian in 1983.

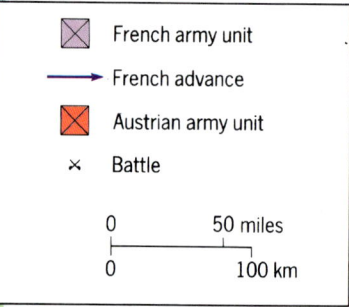

40 THE FRENCH REVOLUTION

B

A painting of Napoleon going through the Great St Bernard Pass.

Painted by Jacques Louis David in 1800. This artist was Napoleon's 'official' painter.

SOURCE

The Battle of Marengo

Napoleon attacked the Austrians near the village of **Marengo**. He had an army of 40,000 men. He hoped to take the Austrians by surprise.

Questions

1 Read **Source A**.
   How did Napoleon cross the Great St Bernard Pass?

2 Look at **Source B**.
   a How is Napoleon shown in the painting?
   b Why do you think he is shown like this?

A lucky victory

Napoleon's army was tired after the long journey. Napoleon split up his army. He sent some of his soldiers away from the battlefield with **General Desaix**. The idea was to cut off the battlefield so the Austrians could not escape.

Napoleon stayed to fight. The Austrians had 30,000 men. They now outnumbered the French.
They began to win the battle.

Then, just in time, General Desaix returned. He was helped by the cavalry of **General Kellerman**. Together they made all the difference and the Austrians were beaten. Desaix was killed in the battle.

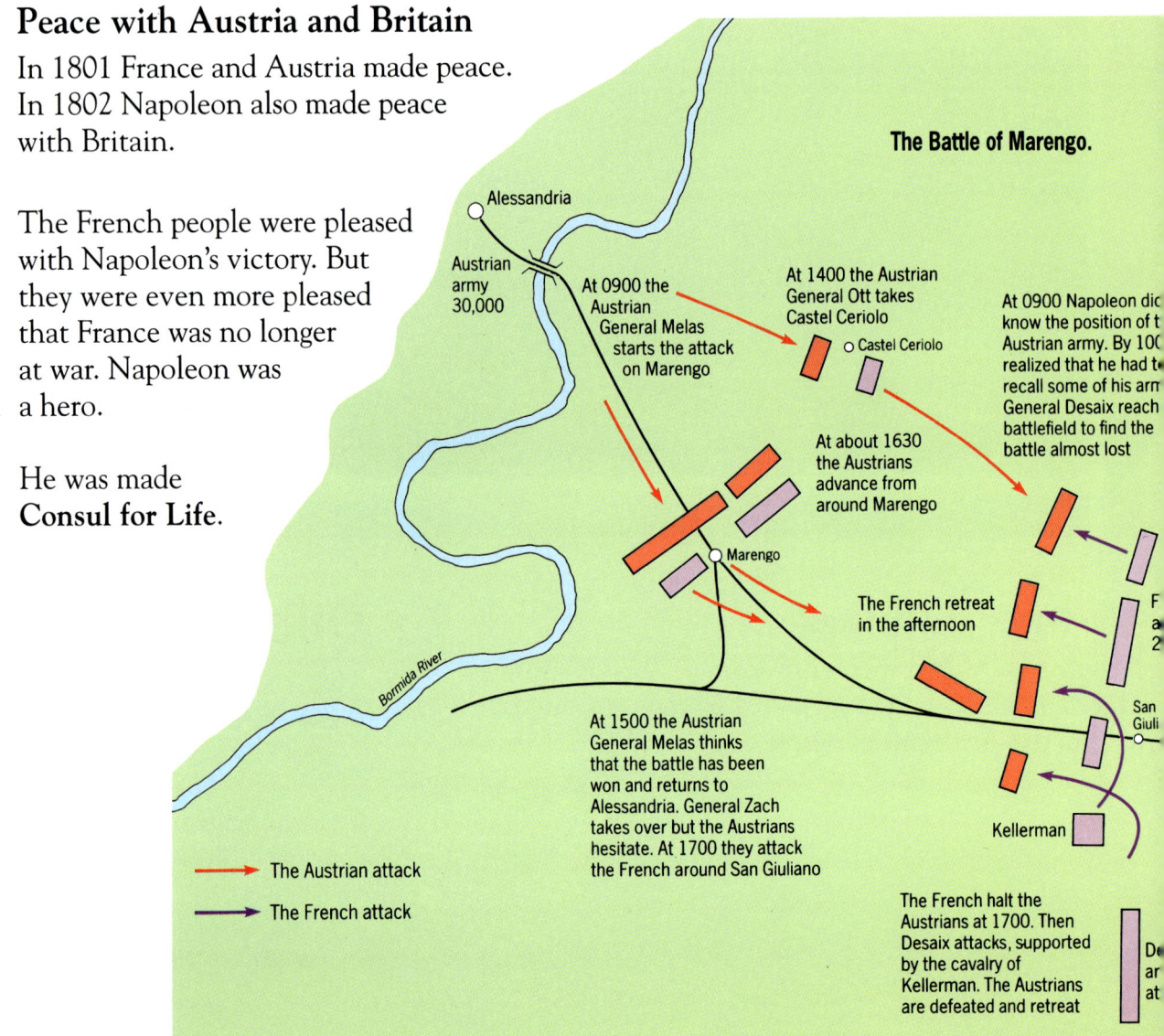

Peace with Austria and Britain

In 1801 France and Austria made peace. In 1802 Napoleon also made peace with Britain.

The French people were pleased with Napoleon's victory. But they were even more pleased that France was no longer at war. Napoleon was a hero.

He was made **Consul for Life**.

The Battle of Marengo.

Alessandria

Austrian army 30,000

At 0900 the Austrian General Melas starts the attack on Marengo

At 1400 the Austrian General Ott takes Castel Ceriolo

Castel Ceriolo

At 0900 Napoleon did know the position of t Austrian army. By 10(realized that he had t recall some of his arm General Desaix reach battlefield to find the battle almost lost

At about 1630 the Austrians advance from around Marengo

Marengo

The French retreat in the afternoon

Bormida River

At 1500 the Austrian General Melas thinks that the battle has been won and returns to Alessandria. General Zach takes over but the Austrians hesitate. At 1700 they attack the French around San Giuliano

San Giuli

Kellerman

→ The Austrian attack
→ The French attack

The French halt the Austrians at 1700. Then Desaix attacks, supported by the cavalry of Kellerman. The Austrians are defeated and retreat

C

The Battle of Marengo, painted by a French artist. Napoleon is in the middle of the picture.

D Napoleon played little part in the victory at Marengo. He did not even arrive until two hours after the start of the battle. He thought he would win easily. The battle was won by Desaix and Kellerman, but they have only received a little praise.

Written by a historian in 1980.

E Desaix arrived at 5pm. He attacked the Austrians. They fell back. Desaix died but Kellerman charged the Austrians. They were beaten.

Written by a historian in 1979.

Questions

1 Read **A lucky victory** and **Source E**.
   How did General Desaix help to win the Battle of Marengo?

2 Now read **Source D**.
   'Napoleon did very little to win the battle.' Do you agree? Explain your answer.

3 Read **Peace**. Copy and complete these sentences.
   In 1801_____.
   In 1802_____.
   The French people looked upon Napoleon as a_____. He was made_____.

THE FRENCH REVOLUTION 43

3.3 Invasion Britain

France and Britain at war again!

After only six months of peace, France and Britain went back to war. The British were angry that Napoleon had gone on capturing land. They knew Napoleon wanted to build a big empire.

Napoleon was angry with Britain. It was sheltering nobles who had fled from France. He decided to **invade Britain**.

The two sides

Britain
France

Britain and France in 1804.

Strong navy – 52 ships
Small army
Nelson was a good admiral

Strong army – 150,000 men
Small navy
Napoleon was a good general

A SOURCE

The French admirals knew it would be hard to invade Britain by sea. The English Channel had dangerous currents.

The British navy was also stronger than the French navy.

Napoleon took no notice of this. He said the French army would row across the Channel in a fleet of boats.

But these boats were small and easy to sink.

Written by a British historian in 1978.

B SOURCE

A Martello tower. Many of these were built by the British to defend the country from the French.

C

SOURCE

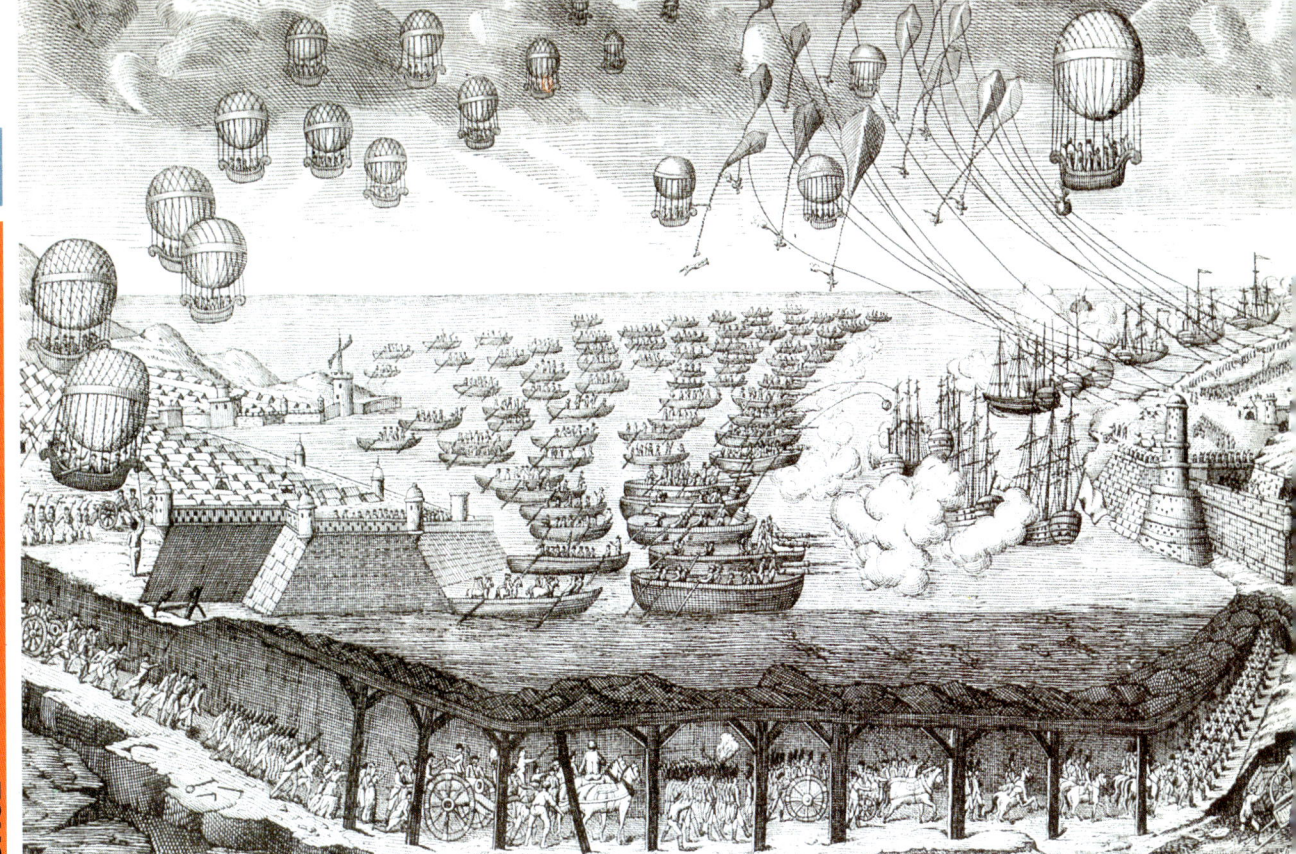

A cartoon of 1803. It shows the French army crossing the Channel to England (on the right).

Napoleon prepares for invasion

Napoleon built 2,000 boats to carry the French army across the Channel. An army of 200,000 men gathered on the north coast of France. If the weather was good, the army planned to cross the Channel in January 1804. Good weather did not arrive.

The Battle of Trafalgar 1805

The French navy wanted to beat the British navy. The French navy would then control the Channel and the troops could cross without being attacked.

In October 1805 the French and British navies fought the **Battle of Trafalgar**. The French navy was destroyed. Britain's **Lord Nelson** was killed in the battle.

The invasion is called off

Napoleon was now left without a navy. The French soldiers would not have any protection when they crossed the Channel. He had to call off the invasion.

Questions

1. Read **Source A**.
   Why did the French admirals think it would be hard to invade Britain?

2. Read the **Battle of Trafalgar**.
   a What did the French navy want to do?
   b What happened at Trafalgar?

3. Read **The invasion is called off**.
   Why did Napoleon call off the invasion?

THE FRENCH REVOLUTION 45

3.4 The New Caesar?

Emperor of France

In 1804 Napoleon crowned himself **Emperor of France**. He had won many battles and built up an empire for France.

Napoleon wanted people to think he was a great man.
He ordered paintings to be done showing him as a great man.

Napoleon had read about the Roman emperors. He wanted to be like the first Roman emperor, **Caesar Augustus**.

A *A drinking cup from Gaul (France, conquered by the Romans). It shows an emperor driving through Rome in triumph. Emperors did this after winning a battle.*

B *Constantine's Arch from Ancient Rome.*

C *L'Arc de Triomphe du Carrousel in Paris. It was started in 1806 and has carvings of Napoleon's victories.*

D You must not die without leaving things for people to remember you by.

SOURCE

Napoleon explaining why he built canals, roads and large public buildings.

E
- I fought many wars all over the world.
- I brought peace to many countries.
- I added Egypt to the Roman Empire.

SOURCE

The Roman emperor, Caesar Augustus, writing about some of the things he did.

F

SOURCE

A French painting showing Napoleon going up to heaven.

Questions

1 Look at **Source B** and **Source C**.
  a In what ways are they similar?
  b Why do you think they are similar?

2 Look at **Source F**.
  a Make a copy of this chart.
  b Answer the questions about Source F.

Questions	Source F
What is it?	
How is Napoleon shown?	
Why might he be shown like this?	

3.5 The Crowning of the New Caesar

Jacques Louis David (1748–1825) – French painter

David knew a lot about the art and sculpture of the Ancient Romans.

David was a supporter of the French Revolution.
He painted many scenes from the Revolution (see page 15).
He agreed with the execution of Louis XVI in 1793.

David supported Robespierre.
He only just escaped the guillotine after Robespierre's death.

Napoleon liked his work.
David called Napoleon his 'hero' (see page 41).

B David made a sketch of Napoleon crowning himself Emperor. He showed Napoleon holding a sword against his heart.

David said this showed the sword had helped Napoleon to win the crown and it would help him to defend it.

In truth, Napoleon did not hold a sword when he crowned himself.

Written by a historian in 1983.

A The painting of Napoleon's coronation by David, 1805–7.

C SOURCE

Sketch by David for the painting of the coronation of Napoleon.

Napoleon makes David his chief painter

Napoleon made David his chief painter in 1804. Napoleon told David to paint pictures which showed him as a great man and a brave soldier.
People would look at the paintings and be impressed.

Napoleon's coronation

Napoleon crowned himself emperor in the cathedral of **Notre Dame** in Paris. France was no longer a republic. It was a **monarchy** again – like it had been before the Revolution. David was told to do a painting of the coronation.

David's painting of the coronation

The painting is shown in Source B. Its size is nine metres by six metres. Several things in it are made up:

1 Napoleon told David to show the Pope with raised hands. This was to make it look as though he was blessing the coronation.
2 Napoleon's mother is shown sitting in the middle of the painting. In truth she was not even there!
3 Only two members of David's family were invited to the coronation. He was so angry he painted all of his family into the picture! They are shown above Napoleon's mother.

Questions

1 Read **Napoleon makes David his chief painter**.
   a How did Napoleon want David to show him in paintings?
   b Why did he want this?

2 Read the box about **David** and look back to pages 46–7. Would Napoleon have liked the fact that David knew about Roman art? Explain your answer.

3 'A lot of Source B is made up and is useless as evidence about Napoleon's coronation.' Do you agree? Explain your answer.

THE FRENCH REVOLUTION 49

3.6 The Great Reformer

Napoleon tried to **reform** (improve) France.

Napoleon gave these medals to people who worked hard.

Education

Napoleon built more schools. — Science and Maths were made more important than before.

The Code Napoleon 1804

This was a list of laws made by Napoleon.

- no special rights for nobles or churchmen.

- all people were equal before the law.

- trial by jury.

- everyone allowed to worship as they wanted.

- women could only own property with the permission of their husbands.

- children could be put in prison by their fathers.

These rules were used in France and other countries which Napoleon conquered, such as Spain, Italy and parts of Germany.

A SOURCE

B SOURCE

You must win the trust of the people.

You must use the Code Napoleon and trial by jury.

Napoleon gave this advice to his brother when he became King of Westphalia.

50 THE FRENCH REVOLUTION

C

The view along the Rue de Rivoli, Paris, built after Napoleon was crowned Emperor.

D

A bride is under the protection of her husband.

She must ask her husband when she wants to go to the theatre. Women should stick to knitting.

Said by Napoleon in 1804.

No free speech

Newspapers could only print good things about Napoleon.

Napoleon used secret police to arrest people.

Buildings

Napoleon built new roads, canals and bridges. He also put up many large buildings in Paris.

E

Napoleon only helped the workers with one thing. This was keeping the price of bread down.

Napoleon thought that hungry people started revolutions.

Written by a historian in 1983.

Questions

1. List five things Napoleon did to **improve** France.

2. Would everyone in France have liked Napoleon's changes? Explain your answer.

3. Read **Source E** and **No free speech**. How did Napoleon control the French people?

3.7 Master of Europe

A huge empire

By 1810 Napoleon had built a huge empire (see map). Only seven countries in Europe were not ruled by France.

The Continental System

Britain was Napoleon's most dangerous enemy. He now realized that it would be too difficult to invade Britain (see pages 44-5).

In 1806 he introduced the **Continental System**. All countries under Napoleon's control were banned from buying British goods.

Napoleon hoped to ruin British trade. Then Britain would be bankrupt and would have to surrender.

The plan failed. Some countries did not obey Napoleon. Those which did were **blockaded** by the British navy. It stopped goods going in. Soon these countries were without coffee, sugar and tobacco.

Napoleon's victories

1805

Austria and Russia beaten at the **Battle of Austerlitz**.

1806

Prussia beaten at the **Battle of Jena**.

1807

Napoleon made Russia and Prussia sign the **Treaty of Tilsit**. Prussia lost one-third of its land.

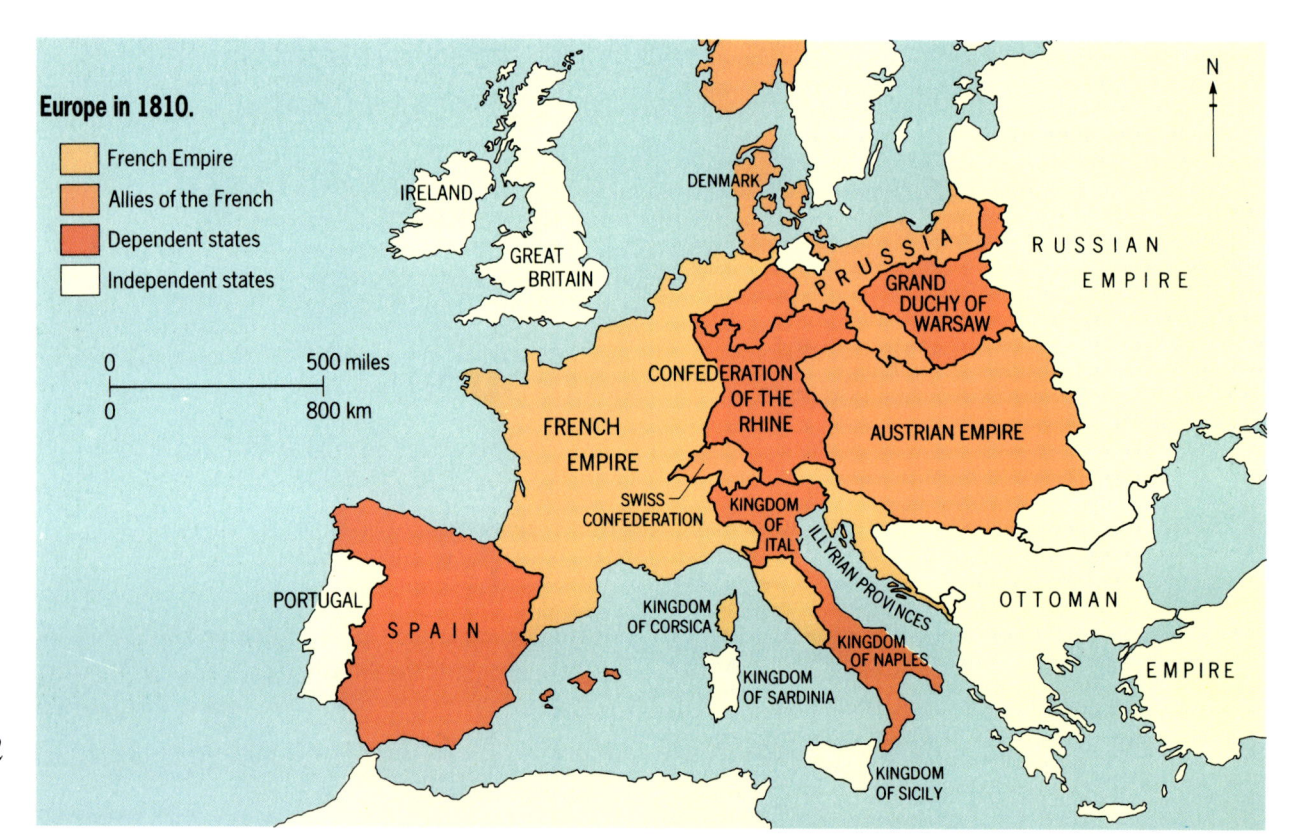

Europe in 1810.
- French Empire
- Allies of the French
- Dependent states
- Independent states

A SOURCE

English cartoon, 1808, showing opinions about Napoleon held by people in different countries.

B SOURCE

Napoleon was starting to worry. He knew he only kept control of countries by force. He said that one defeat would end his career.

Written by a British historian in 1989.

The Continental System

Blockade by British navy

Trafalgar 1805

The British navy blockaded any country which refused to trade with Britain.

Questions

1 Look at the map. List the countries which were **not** controlled by Napoleon in 1810.

2 Read **The Continental System**.
   a What was it?
   b Why did Napoleon introduce it?
   c Why did it fail?

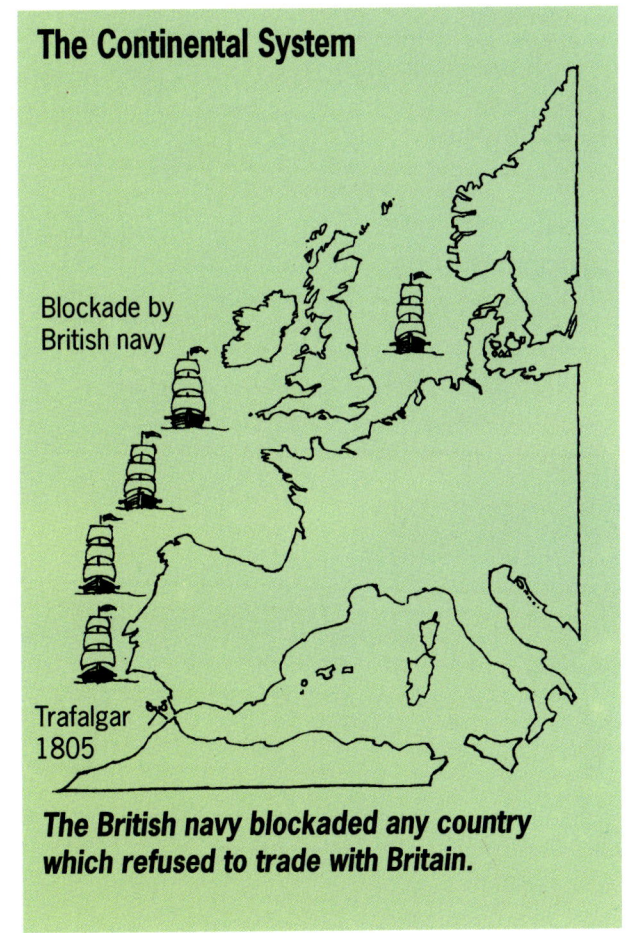

THE FRENCH REVOLUTION 53

4.1 The Peninsular War

Why did it start?

Portugal and **Spain** make up the Peninsular. Portugal traded a lot with Britain. Napoleon wanted to bring Portugal under the Continental System. This would stop Portugal trading with Britain. Portugal did not want this to happen.

In 1808 Napoleon marched through Spain and invaded Portugal. Napoleon made his brother, **Joseph**, the King of Spain. The Spanish did not want him as their king.

Both the Spanish and the Portuguese were angry. They rose up in revolt against the French. This was the **Peninsular War**. It lasted until 1813. Britain sent an army to help Spain and Portugal.

Problems for France

1 Troops and money

The French were beaten by the Spanish at **Baylen** (see map). Napoleon was forced to send 300,000 men to fight in Spain and Portugal. He could have done with these troops in other places where he was fighting. Napoleon said this was his 'Spanish ulcer' because it cost a lot of men and money.

A Both sides did terrible things.

The French chopped up dead bodies. They strung them up as a warning to other rebels.

Goya did a drawing to show his horror at how dead men were butchered and hung.

A description of what is shown in Source B. Written by a historian in 1983.

The Peninsular War.

B SOURCE

A drawing done in 1810 by the Spanish artist, Francisco Goya.

2 Guerilla warfare

The Spanish did not fight big battles against the French. They would have been beaten. Instead small groups of peasants would hide in the mountains and ambush the French. They would kill as many French soldiers as they could and then run off into hiding. This was called **guerilla warfare**. The French were unable to do much about it.

3 The Duke of Wellington

Things became even worse when the British army arrived in Portugal. It was commanded by Sir Arthur Wellesley. In 1809 he beat the French in the **Battle of Talavera**. After this he was made the **Duke of Wellington**.

Napoleon is beaten

In 1812 Napoleon had to take men from Spain **to fight in Russia**. This made his army in Spain very weak. Wellington pushed the French army back into France. Napoleon had lost the Peninsular War.

Questions

1. Read **Why did it start?**
   a. Why was Spain angry with Napoleon?
   b. Why was Portugal angry with Napoleon?

2. Read **Problems for France**. Copy and complete these sentences:
   a. The war cost France a lot of _____ and ____.
   b. The Spanish used _____ warfare.
   c. The British sent the _____ of _____ to help the Spanish.

3. Why do you think Napoleon called the war his 'Spanish ulcer'?

4.2 The Invasion of Russia

Why Napoleon invaded Russia

Russia was under the Continental System. It was not allowed to trade with Britain. The **Tsar** (King) of Russia said his people could not do without British goods. So Russia left the Continental System. This made Napoleon angry. He decided to invade Russia to teach the Russians a lesson. It turned out to be a big mistake.

Napoleon invades

In June 1812 Napoleon invaded Russia with an army of 600,000. He called it the **Grand Army**. But the invasion was badly planned. Silly mistakes were made.

Mistakes

1 **No winter clothes**: Napoleon said he would conquer Russia in a month. But it took weeks to invade!
He had forgotten that Russia was such a huge country, which had very cold winters. The freezing Russian winter set in.
The French army, though, had not brought any winter uniforms!

2 **No supplies**: It was hard to transport enough food to such a big army over such a long way. So the French said they would eat corn from the fields and gather fruit. But the Russians retreated in front of the French. As they went they burnt everything they thought the French could eat or use. This is called a **scorched earth** policy. It left the French short of food.

The Tsar

- The Tsar was the King of Russia.
- He did not trust Napoleon.
- He wanted to beat Napoleon and was not worried how long it might take.

A SOURCE

The Russians burnt crops as they retreated.

B SOURCE

The French army was past its best.

It had been fighting for 19 years and was tired.

It was getting hard to find good officers.

Young boys were called up to keep up numbers.

The generals wanted peace.

Written by a historian in 1979.

Moscow was 2,000 miles from Paris.

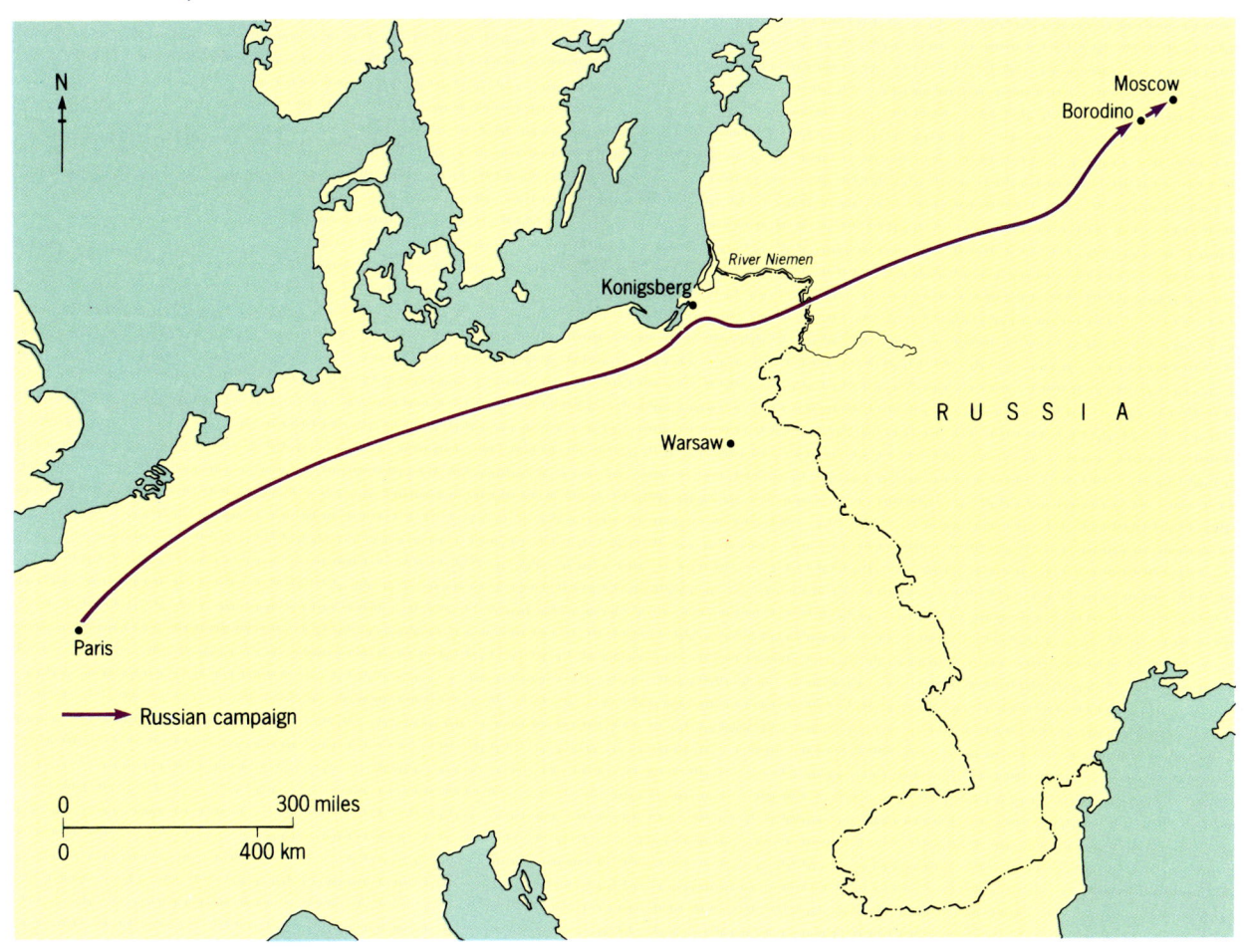

The Battle of Borodino

On 7 September 1812 the French beat the Russians in the Battle of Borodino. Both sides had many men killed.

The French then marched into Moscow. It was deserted. All the Russian people had left.

Fire!

Then the city mysteriously went up in flames.
Napoleon's army now had no shelter and no food.
There was nothing for it but to retreat.

Questions

1 Read **Why Napoleon invaded Russia**.
   Why was Napoleon angry with the Tsar?

2 Read **Mistakes**.
   a What had Napoleon forgotten about Russia?
   b What did this mean for his army?
   c What was the scorched earth policy?

3 Read **Fire!**
   a What happened when the French reached Moscow?
   b What did this mean for the French?

4.3 Retreat from Moscow

A long journey back

Many soldiers died on the long march back to France.

They died of starvation, frostbite and disease. Others were ambushed and killed by the Russians.

Only 20,000 men made it back to France.

Sources A–E give different views about why the invasion failed.

A We were beaten by the cold winter. I stayed too long in Moscow. I should have left four days after I entered it. Then the Russians would have been lost.

Napoleon said this to one of his generals.

Napoleon's army retreating. A painting of 1812.

B

58 THE FRENCH REVOLUTION

C We failed because:
Our wagons were not strong enough.

There were no horses to steal from the Russians. We could not pull the wagons. The Russians had fled and taken their horses with them.

We had to leave wagons at the side of the road. We could not transport our supplies.

Said by the Duke of Vicenza, 1812–13.

D The French army lost 350,000 men on the way to Moscow and only 80,000 when retreating. Many men had already died before the really bad weather set in.

Many horses died of overwork and hunger before the cold came.

A British historian, 1978.

E A commander who cares for his army will not make his men march in winter or make the horses work too hard.

The Duke of Wellington's view about why Napoleon failed in Russia.

Questions

1. Look at **Source B** and read **A long journey back**.
   What does the artist of Source B want people to think about Napoleon's retreat?

2. **a** Make a large copy of the chart below.

Source	Why Napoleon failed
A	
C	
D	
E	

   b Complete the chart by writing in what each source says about the reasons for Napoleon's failure.

3. 'Napoleon failed because the invasion was badly planned.'
   Do you agree with this view? (It will help to look back to pages 56–7.)

4.4 Defeat and Abdication

Napoleon in trouble

1 Many countries thought that Napoleon could be beaten once and for all. Britain, Russia, Prussia, Austria and Sweden joined together to fight Napoleon. It was called a **coalition**.

2 Napoleon was short of money and soldiers.

3 The French people did not want any more fighting. The wars had put food in short supply.

Boy soldiers

Napoleon foolishly decided to keep fighting. But he had lost so many soldiers he had to get young boys to join the army. They were untrained.

Defeat at Leipzig 1813

Napoleon fought the coalition countries at **Leipzig**. He was badly beaten. Foreign armies now marched on France.

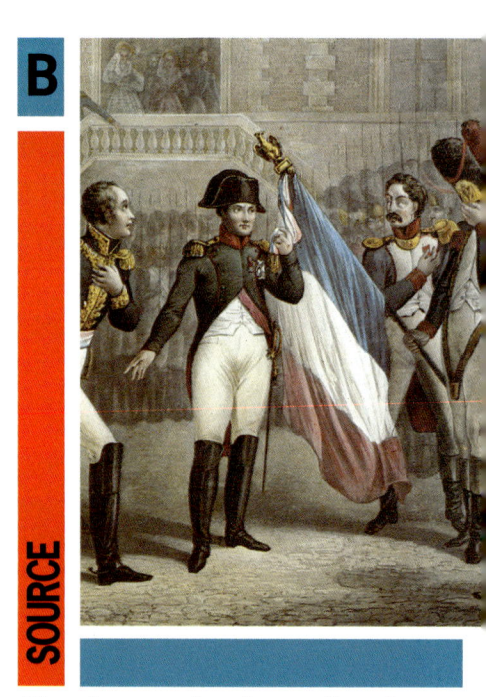

B SOURCE

Napoleon saying farewell to the French army in 1814.

A SOURCE

A British cartoon, 1814.
It shows Napoleon on his way to Elba. The British were pleased to see the back of him.

C SOURCE

A drawing by a French artist. It shows Napoleon with his boy soldiers.

D SOURCE

His decision to fight on in 1814 instead of making peace was foolish. He had only 60,000 troops to fight 200,000 coalition troops.

It was criminal to send young boys into battle.

Said by a British historian, 1978.

E I am one of those men who triumphs or dies.

Said by Napoleon, 1813.

Napoleon gives up the throne

In 1814 the Russian army reached Paris. Napoleon **abdicated** (gave up the throne).

Napoleon sent to Elba

Napoleon was sent to Elba, a small island in the Mediterranean Sea. He was given £200,000 per year.

The royal family returns

Louis XVI's brother went back to France. He was crowned **Louis XVIII**. France had a king once again.

Questions

1. Read **Napoleon in trouble** and **Source D**.
   Why was it foolish for Napoleon to go on fighting?

2. a What did the artist of Source C want people to think about the boy soldiers?
   b Why do you think he wanted people to think this?

3. What happened to Napoleon in 1814?

4.5 The Hundred Days

Napoleon returns to France

Napoleon was bored on the island of Elba. He heard stories from France that the people did not like Louis XVIII.

On 1 March 1815 he escaped from Elba and made his way back to France.

The Battle of Waterloo

The other countries were very worried at Napoleon's return. They gathered a huge army and fought Napoleon at the **Battle of Waterloo**. Napoleon was beaten. His return had lasted a **hundred days**.

A SOURCE

I fought fifty battles and won almost all of them.

I brought in laws which will always carry my name [The Code Napoleon].

I raised myself from nothing to become the most powerful ruler in the world.

If I had succeeded I would have been known as the greatest man who ever lived.

Said by Napoleon just before his death.

B SOURCE

A French painting of Napoleon looking down on his grave from heaven.

62 THE FRENCH REVOLUTION

Europe in 1815.
— German Confederation
▨ Areas of military frontiers

The new Europe

The winning countries met in Vienna. A new map of Europe was drawn. Old rulers were returned to power. France was to be ruled by a king again.

The end of Napoleon

This time Napoleon was sent to the island of St Helena. This was a long way from France in the south Atlantic Ocean. He would not be able to escape from there.

Napoleon died from stomach cancer in 1821.

Questions

1 Read **Napoleon returns to France**.
   What drove Napoleon to escape from Elba?

2 **a** Which battle ended Napoleon's career?
   b When and where did he die?

3 Read **Source A**.
   Which of these statements is true
   - Napoleon was sorry because he had failed.
   - Napoleon was proud of his life and the things he had done?

THE FRENCH REVOLUTION 63

INDEX

Aboukir Bay, Battle of 37
absolute monarchy 4, 5, 8
architecture 30, 46, 51
assignat 20
Austerlitz, Battle of 52
Austria 5, 10, 22, 26, 28, 37, 40, 41, 43, 52, 60

Bastille 16, 17, 18, 34, 35
Baylen 54
Borodino, Battle of 57
bread 12, 14, 16, 18, 26, 27, 32, 51
Britain 5, 22, 26, 37, 44, 52–3, 60
    invasion of 44–5, 52

Catherine the Great 5
Church 6–7, 15, 20
Coalition 60, 62
Code Napoleon 50
Committee of Public Safety 27, 28
Constitution 14–15, 20
Continental System 52–3, 54, 56

David, Jacques Louis 15, 41, 48, 49
Desaix, General 42, 43
Directory 36, 38
    overthrow of 39

education 50
Egyptian campaign 37
emigrés 22
empire, French 46, 52
Estates General 14–15

fashion 30–1
Fleury, Cardinal 9
food crisis 14–15, 16, 23
Frederick the Great 4

gabelle 6
George III 5
Grand Army 56–7, 58

guerilla warfare 55
guillotine 28–9

Habsburg family 5
Holland 26
Hundred Days, the 62–3

India 5, 37
Italy 37, 40

Jena, Battle of 52
Joseph II, Emperor 5

Louis XIV 8, 9
Louis XV 9
Louis XVI 4, 10, 12, 14–15, 16–17, 24, 25, 61
    brought back to Paris 18–19
    execution of 24
    financial crisis 12–13, 14–15
    flight to Varennes 22
Louis XVIII 61, 62

Marengo, Battle of 40–1, 42–3
Marie Antoinette 10, 11, 22, 28, 40
Mazarin, Jules 8
Moscow campaign 56–7, 58–9

Napoleon 36–40, 41–3, 47, 53, 54, 55, 60
    abdication 61
    crowned 39, 46, 49
    early life 36
    empire 52
    exile 61, 63
    hundred days 62–3
    invasion of Britain 44–5
    invasion of Russia 56–9
    Napoleonic code 50
    reforms 50–1
    seizes power 38–9
National Assembly 15, 16, 18, 20, 22

National Convention 26
Nelson, Lord 37, 44, 45
nobility 6, 12, 14, 15, 18, 20, 22

peasants 6, 7, 14, 55–6
Peninsular War 54–5
Portugal 54, 55
Prussia 4, 22, 26, 52, 60
Pyramids, Battle of the 37, 39
Pyrenees, Battle of the 55

Reign of Terror 26–9
Republic 24
revolutionary ideas 22
riots 14
Robespierre 27, 28–9, 36, 48
Russia 5, 52, 55, 56–7, 58–9, 60

Sans culottes 22, 30
scorched earth policy 56
September Massacres 22
Seven Years' War 9
Spain 26, 54–5, 57

Talavera, Battle of 55
taxation 6, 7, 12–14, 18, 20
taxes
    gabelle 6, 20
    taille 6
    tithes 6, 18
Tennis Court Oath 15, 34
The Terror 26–29, 30
three estates 6, 14–15
Tilsit, Treaty of 52
Toulon 36
Trafalgar, Battle of 45
Tsar, of Russia 56

Versailles 8–9, 18

war of 1792 22
Waterloo, Battle of 62
Wellington, Duke of 55, 59